CONCERT FAVORITES

Volume 1

Band Arrangements Correlated with Essential Elements Band Method Book 1

ISBN 978-0-634-05201-9

7777 W. BLUEMOUND RD. P.O. BOX 13819 MILWAUKEE, WI 53213

Copyright © 2002 by HAL LEONARD CORPORATION
International Copyright Secured   All Rights Reserved

LET'S ROCK!

BASSOON

MICHAEL SWEENEY (ASCAP)

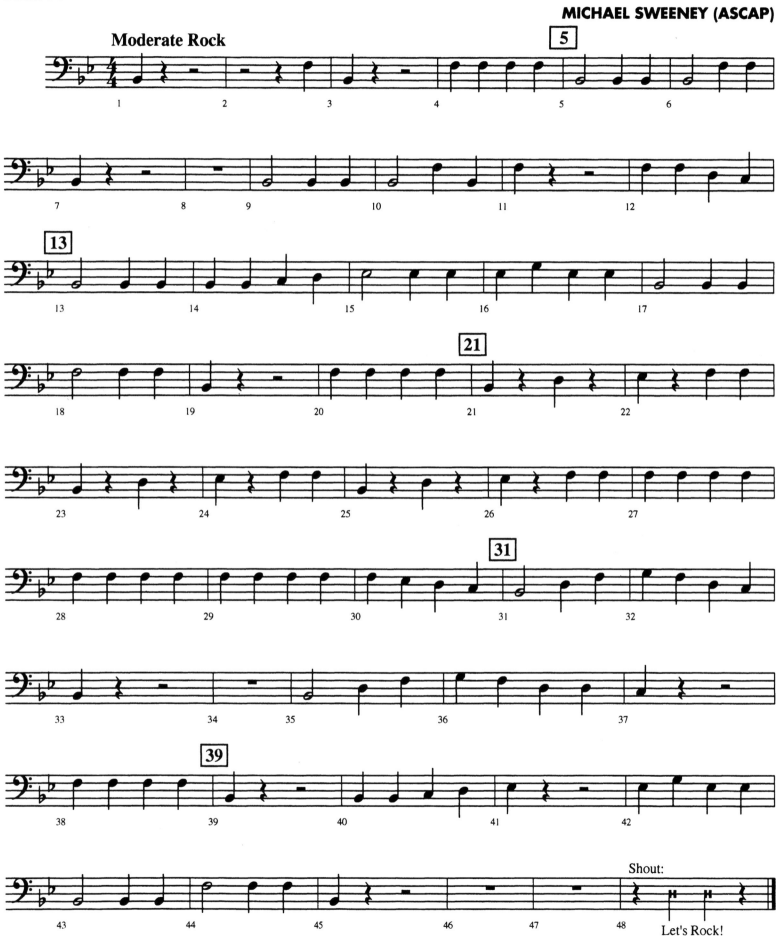

Copyright © 1995 by HAL LEONARD CORPORATION
International Copyright Secured All Rights Reserved

00860121

MAJESTIC MARCH

BASSOON

By PAUL LAVENDER

Copyright © 1997 by HAL LEONARD CORPORATION
International Copyright Secured   All Rights Reserved

00860121

MICKEY MOUSE MARCH
(From Walt Disney's "THE MICKEY MOUSE CLUB")

BASSOON

Words and Music by JIMMIE DODD
Arranged by MICHAEL SWEENEY

© 1955 Walt Disney Music Company
Copyright Renewed
This arrangement © 1992 Walt Disney Music Company
All Rights Reserved   Used by Permission

00860121

POWER ROCK
(We Will Rock You • Another One Bites The Dust)

BASSOON

Arranged by MICHAEL SWEENEY

WE WILL ROCK YOU
Words and Music by BRIAN MAY
© 1977 QUEEN MUSIC LTD.
This arrangement © 1992 QUEEN MUSIC LTD.
All Rights Controlled and Administered by BEECHWOOD MUSIC CORP.
All Rights Reserved   International Copyright Reserved
Used by Permission

ANOTHER ONE BITES THE DUST
Words and Music by JOHN DEACON
© 1980 QUEEN MUSIC LTD.
This arrangement © 1992 QUEEN MUSIC LTD.
All Rights Controlled and Administered by BEECHWOOD MUSIC CORP.
All Rights Reserved   International Copyright Reserved
Used by Permission

00860121

WHEN THE SAINTS GO MARCHING IN

Words by KATHERINE E. PURVIS
Music by JAMES M. BLACK
Arranged by JOHN HIGGINS

BASSOON

00860121

Copyright ©1994 by HAL LEONARD CORPORATION
International Copyright Secured All Rights Reserved

FARANDOLE
(From "L'Arlésienne")

GEORGES BIZET
Arranged by MICHAEL SWEENEY (ASCAP)

BASSOON

Copyright © 1993 by HAL LEONARD CORPORATION
International Copyright Secured   All Rights Reserved

00860121

JUS' PLAIN BLUES

BASSOON

MICHAEL SWEENEY (ASCAP)

Copyright © 1994 by HAL LEONARD CORPORATION
International Copyright Secured   All Rights Reserved

From the Paramount and Twentieth Century Fox Motion Picture TITANIC

MY HEART WILL GO ON
(Love Theme From 'Titanic')

Music by JAMES HORNER
Lyric by WILL JENNINGS
Arranged by PAUL LAVENDER

BASSOON

Copyright © 1997 by Famous Music Corporation, Ensign Music Corporation, TCF Music Publishing, Inc., Fox Film Music Corporation and Blue Sky Rider Songs
This arrangement Copyright © 1998 by Famous Music Corporation, Ensign Music Corporation,
TCF Music Publishing, Inc., Fox Film Music Corporation and Blue Sky Rider Songs
All Rights for Blue Sky Rider Songs Administered by Irving Music, Inc.
International Copyright Secured   All Rights Reserved

From THE MUPPET MOVIE

THE RAINBOW CONNECTION

Words and Music by PAUL WILLIAMS
and KENNITH L. ASCHER
Arranged by PAUL LAVENDER

BASSOON

Copyright © 1979 Jim Henson Productions, Inc.
This arrangement Copyright © 1998 Jim Henson Productions, Inc.
All Rights Administered by Sony/ATV Music Publishing, 8 Music Square West, Nashville, TN 37203
International Copyright Secured   All Rights Reserved

From Walt Disney's MARY POPPINS
SUPERCALIFRAGILISTICEXPIALIDOCIOUS

Words and Music by
RICHARD M. SHERMAN and ROBERT B. SHERMAN
Arranged by MICHAEL SWEENEY

Bassoon

© 1963 Wonderland Music Company, Inc.
Copyright Renewed
This arrangement © 2000 Wonderland Music, Inc.
All Rights Reserved   Used by Permission

(From "THE SOUND OF MUSIC")

DO-RE-MI

BASSOON

Lyrics by **OSCAR HAMMERSTEIN II**
Music by **RICHARD RODGERS**
Arranged by PAUL LAVENDER

Copyright © 1959 by Richard Rodgers and Oscar Hammerstein II
Copyright Renewed
This arrangement Copyright © 1993 by WILLIAMSON MUSIC
WILLIAMSON MUSIC owner of publication and allied rights throughout the world
International Copyright Secured   All Rights Reserved

DRUMS OF CORONA

BASSOON

MICHAEL SWEENEY (ASCAP)

Copyright © 1998 by HAL LEONARD CORPORATION
International Copyright Secured   All Rights Reserved

00860121

LAREDO
(Concert March)

BASSOON

JOHN HIGGINS

Copyright © 1994 by HAL LEONARD CORPORATION
International Copyright Secured   All Rights Reserved

POMP AND CIRCUMSTANCE
March No. 1

By EDWARD ELGAR
Arranged by MICHAEL SWEENEY

BASSOON

Copyright © 1997 by HAL LEONARD CORPORATION
International Copyright Secured   All Rights Reserved

00860121

STRATFORD MARCH

BASSOON

JOHN HIGGINS (ASCAP)

Copyright © 1995 by HAL LEONARD CORPORATION
International Copyright Secured   All Rights Reserved

00860121